AF353855

BEREAVEMENT

The Do's and Don'ts of helping people who are grieving

DEE. R. BANNER

Tulip Publications
"bring concepts to life"
Ceintuurbaan 23B
Rotterdam The Netherlands
Reach out to us - info@tulippublication.com
Visit our websites - www.tulippublications.com

Contents

Author's Acknowledgements

I would first thank God for trusting me to write this booklet

My family for your patience and love

My children Admira, Aaron, Pierre. I love you so much. I admire your strength and grace through the pain you have endured

My brothers and sisters for believing I can do this

My mum whose strength and wisdom knows no bounds

To my church family, your prayers and support have sustained me

Pastor Ade D'Almeida thank you, thank you, thank you for your love, correction, covering, late night/early morning conversations that kept despair away from me

Carmen Adams my destiny helper, God will richly bless you

My prayer partners (you know who you are) I love respect and honour you

Last but not least, my precious grandchildren, you are for signs and wonders.

Introduction/A Foreword

Before we start, I decided to write this book-let after experiencing the passing to glory of my husband. We shared over twenty years of marriage together.

Through the weeks, months and first year, it became clear to me that although people were well-meaning, knowing how to comfort the bereaved was not a gift many people possessed. Often there were times their words were outright insulting and insensitive.

I hope this booklet offers help to all those involved in the bereavement process whether you are the bereaved, a friend, family member or work colleague.

For the bereaved, no matter how the loss of a loved one happened, I would like these words to help you as you make sense of what you are going through.

There are so many emotions, thoughts, decisions to be made, questions to be asked and answered. I encourage you to see that you do not need to rush into making a decision. If you need to, close your door and see no one for a while (though I would not advise too long a period on your own).

For those who are connected to the bereaved person, this advice will put you in a better position to guide and be of greater assistance to the bereaved and those around them. It can be used to help your loved one or friend carry on with as little outside distraction as possible.

⊱ X ⊰

The points from each section are important as these may be some of the things you have had to deal with through the bereavement process and I believe all the points in this booklet are for correction, understanding, and clarity.

I believe I coped through this very traumatic time because of my faith and my children.

Please do not misunderstand me I am not super woman but, I am a woman of faith.

I do know myself and so I had to dig deep and tell God "I do not understand. My heart has been broken; my world has changed for ever, what I used to know no longer exists".

One thing I did purpose in my heart and that was not to ask God "Why?".

I told Him "I do know you know all things, and my children have to see you in all of this, they have to see that you have not left them or me."

And this I instructed my children to do, "Under no circumstance ask God why?".

So, I asked God for his help. To help me and to help them.

I also filled the house with worship songs.

I was, and am, very fortunate to be surrounded by a big family and very special friends.

I can honestly say in the first few weeks of loss my family and close friends built a strong wall around me and my children, each one took a role and ran with it. This enabled me to gather strength and prepare to see visitors.

I also give my profound thanks to my church family for their prayers and support.

I cannot express the relief this brought me and my thanks to them for their wisdom and love.

What also helped at this time was the fact my husband and I had discussed years before how we would want things for each other should one of us pass away. This was not only a private discussion as it included our children, so they too were aware of our plans and desires for each other and as a family.

I trust you will find comfort and encouragement as you read.

About the Author

Dee and Eric were married for 28 years before he passed away in 2012.

She lives in London and is the proud mother of three children: Admira, Aaron, and Pierre.

Dee also has four granddaughter's and one grandson all of whom she adores immensely.

In her professional life she works for the Ministry and runs the Business Shecaniah Etiquette School and is a mentor to many. But, her calling and passion is serving on the Mission Field and Prison Ministry.

"Losing someone close to you can be a real shock to the system and can leave everyone at a loss for words. Motivated by her own bereavement, Dee's have written this empowering booklet to give comfort and support to the bereaved and those supporting them."

Carmen Adams

DO

Do listen to the person who is grieving, they may just need to talk

2

Do take time to talk to the children
who have experienced loss

Do offer to help with practical things i.e shopping, take young children out to the park

4

*Do be prepared to sit in silence.
Sometimes the bereaved may need
people around but also like the silence*

5

Do let the grieving person cry

6

Do check if it is ok to visit

*Do be sensitive when visiting the grieving
family and sharing information.
You may not know who you are talking
to and they may not be family*

8

*Do be mindful of being of help
in the area that is needed*

*Do allow the person who is
grieving to ask question*

*Do be prepared to pray with
the person if asked to.*

DO NOT

1

Do not be offended if the grieving person does not want to receive visitors in the early stages

2

Do not tell the grieving person you know how they feel. You may have experienced grief, but every relationship is unique

Do not assume roles that have
not be given to you, E.g. speaking
on behalf of the bereaved

4

Do not inform older children that they have to take the place of the deceased (older brother, sister, mother)

5

Do not visit the bereaved with the intention of seeking information. This is usually picked up the bereaved and will cause more distress

Do not ask pointed questions early on in the bereavement i.e. How are you going to dispose of the deceased belongings?

7

*Do not have an expectation of
how the bereaved should be*

*Do not have a time limit on how you
expect the bereaved to behave*

*Do not express to the bereaved
how you think they or their siblings
or children should be feeling*

Do not try to control or change
arrangements that the bereaved have
already expressed they want.

UNDER NO CIRCUMSTANCE

The below points are an absolute no-no when you are in the position of counselling the bereaved.

1

*Under no circumstance should
you put your cultural views upon
the person who is grieving*

2

*Under no circumstance start discussing
in front of children what your thoughts
are concerning the death of their parent,
brother, sister. Especially if you are not
family or close to the family, this can cause
more hurt or confusion for them depending
on their age and information they have
been given by the person who knows best*

3

*Under no circumstance express offence
if the grieving person does not want
to talk during the grieving process*

4

*Under no circumstance is it acceptable to
contact the bereaved if they have asked to
be left alone for a while or not to call them*

*Under no circumstance put pressure
on the person who is grieving to be
a part of practices that are not in line
with their faith or belief system*

6

*Under no circumstance make phone
calls to the grieving family with your
own personal theories and hear says*

Under no circumstance is it ok to put pressure on the bereaved to return to work

8

*Under no circumstance make
known to others information that
has been entrusted to you*

*Under no circumstance is it ok for
you to misguide the bereaved with
information that is not true or confirmed*

Under no circumstance is it ok for you to change arrangements or details regarding the burial, service, or family plans without consulting the bereaved first.

www.ingramcontent.com/pod-product-compliance
Lightning Source LLC
LaVergne TN
LVHW021209200726
843509LV00010B/882